Quaker

Minims

Quaker Minims

BY

Eric H. Edwards

One Bird Books • Hatchville, Mass.

Copyright 2024 @ Eric H. Edwards

ISBN: 978-1-7339200-8-7

One Bird Books • Hatchville, Mass.

Introduction

Of the many titles I considered for this book, I ended up with the word Minims, the word referring to about one drop of liquid. It's appropriate for words appearing out of my Cloud of Unknowing, like tears, or perhaps the fact that I live by the Atlantic ocean. I find the word Quaker to be more precise than the other candidate (Friendly), and a little cooler, befitting the tone of some of the texts. All the statements arose from "worship," whether in meeting or in my solitary practice, a practice exactly the same in both instances. I have found that meetings for worship are not themselves worship and never were intended that way, but rather the possibility that worship might occur in such meetings. Stop and wait. After that it is God's turn to seize the opportunity to be present (or not), a comfort (or not), and after that it is our opportunity to work out what such a visitation might mean or require.

These Minims are meant to be a comfort, in that if they come from the right place, some of them will resonate within the worship experience for you, confirming a true and gentle life-way or path we travel together in the face of the world's trials. An orientation of direction rather than a formula for life.

Each of us must live our lives responding to the Spirit of Truth, or not. It is your particular life that makes up the Witness and Example Friends often like to refer to. In mystical terms, we cannot save, but we can point.

All proceeds from Inwardness;

Inwardness not of the body
or any place
but of the Creation,

where God is.

Quaker

Minims

Making Quakerism
as plain as day –
as clear as light
on a thing.

A solid thing.

The only way
to bear your cross
is to feel pain
and be free in it.

In worship,
emptiness is everything –
your body is everything.

Everyone in the room
is in a larger emptiness.

To accompany God
in this invitation
is like pouring out
the water of love.

You can decide
to step into the river of love,
but it will carry you away.

If God had a plan
God would be a tyrant.

God has no plan,
only the invitation to love,
without coercion.

God has no meaning.
God creates meaning.

We choose meanings
based upon
how we worship.

The Light

It is not brightness
but comprehensiveness –
not intensity
but clarity.

An unobscured emptiness
is not dark,
an unlimited emptiness
is optimistic.

Discernment

Allowing the Light
to show, to disclose,
the condition of a thing.

When the meeting for worship
is silent
we are in unity.

Good vocal ministry
speaks from unity
and into the unity of the meeting.

Being faithful
is not knowing how to seek,
but to wait, alert,
together or alone,
willing to be found.

Speaking is like the wind
so mind your breath.

Action is fire
so mind your body.

The body is dust
but it is completely you.

Words are water
so mind the source.

The Inward Light
saturates the water.

The most restful
thing is to stop
until you have the strength
to take a step.

Do not be afraid
to possess the Light,
and attend its illuminations.

It will go from you
with the same freedom
and manner it surged up
from within you.

The world is a whirlwind.
Are we still of it
or are we quiet within it.

Render unto Caesar

says nothing about money,
everything about your body.

Caesar is also Nature –
all that we are,
we must render
it all to Caesar
the same as Jesus.

Just where might God be?
So where are you?

There is so much
meaning in Nature,
it fills everything –
and it is endlessly
thirsty.

Quaker worship
is silent
either because it is trying
to get out of the way
of God –
or in the way.

The human species is
just one difficulty
of the creation –

our worship
is an attempt to
respond to that
enlightenment.

If there is such a thing
as a moral system

it is because
we all have a mother.

Behold
the lilies of the field,
so sexy, but
their roots invisible.

Stop seeking
so that God
might find you
in this quantum shivering.

Seeking for God
is actually looking
in the wrong direction.

Don't seek for God,
allow God to seek for you.

If you wait
long enough,
you will become
patient.

Goliath
was a part of David,
David better off
for killing him –
you too.

What I experience
I may also own up to –
it is what I possess,
I can speak of it.

What you possess
you may profess
and confess.

If someone speaks
about what they experience,
you do not hear God,
but you may hear in it
what God is also speaking
specifically and Inwardly to you.

Sometimes an entire meeting
is gathered together in the silence
and almost everybody
can affirm it
silently afterwards.

In meeting for worship
you may expect
the entire world
to be made better,
and you may feel
that has happened
even as you rise
from worship understanding
nothing much outwardly
is different.

The invitation
is the One Thing –
what you do with it
are the Ten Thousand Things.

When you give up
certainty
you will recognize
where purity resides.

When you give up
self-sufficiency
you will be in a position to
see
the rock that you stand on.

God wants to be with you,
not somewhere else –
God wants to know you,
not someone else.

When you let God
know you,
you will want to know
someone else.

The more Godlike you are,
the more human you are.

The more Godlike you are,
the more mortal you are.

The more Godlike you are,
the more porous you are.

It is good not to worship
all the time,
so that you can
get something done.

When you have
nothing to say
out in the world,
that is the best time.

The silence of worship
is always waiting,
because it is never absent.

Membership exists
so that within the Society
it is almost nothing –
outside the Society
it is a fearful angel
wielding a fiery sword.

The church
is your body,
is not your body,
is someone else's body.

It is always the case...

The weightier the Friend
the lighter the spirit.

The quieter the Friend
the more the life speaks.

There is only
doing a little better

as a person
in the world.

In worship
there is never
doing better.

Charisma is poison.

Spirituality is
Nothingness.

Worship is
everything.

De Anima

Adult learning is
a consequence of worship.

Everything you know
is because of worship.

Quaker worship is
the most radical worship
human beings can
practice.

Worship in silence has never changed
regardless
of who does it
or where it is done.

On Worship

George Fox said
stop and wait.
More than this is not worship.
Less than this is not worship.

When your life is
meaningful,
worship is meaningless.

When your life is
worthless,
worship is like Gold.

Forgetting God
allows God to be
fully present.

Our unity does not
come about from
or in spite of
our diversity –

Our diversity comes about
because of our unity.

The world
may never be at peace,
but we
may be at peace
with the world.

Quaker evangelizing
is joy –

Quaker proselytizing
is horror.

Quaker confession
is joy –

Quaker demands
are empty.

Quaker submission
is joy –

Quaker insistence
is rude.

Quaker stubbornness
is a result
of submission.

Quaker persuasion
is a result
of Friendship.

It is not that a good cause
is supported
by the worship space,
but the worship space
is supported
by a good cause.

In worship
there is only one community –
Everyone who has lived
Everyone now living
Everyone who will live.

We are born into the middle of things.
As we grow up we begin
to be able to worship in
towards zero.

Then we die in the middle of things.

Sing in the day
for half the good globe
is always in darkness

and

Sing in the night
because half the good globe
is always in daylight.

Acknowledgments

Some acknowledgments are obligatory and easily passed over by a reader looking to get to the text, and some are especially desired by the writer to be made visible, like dedications. My obligation to acknowledge Obadiah Brown's Benevolent Fund (without which there would be no book), comes from me with a particular affection almost as if the Fund were a person who put their arm around me to say we want this book to exist and wish you well with it; may it prove a positive addition to the Quaker experience and some kind of blessing to both of us. Similarly, to Jim Morgan and Mary Kane of One Bird Books (without whom there would be no book).

For the not quite so obligatory acknowledgments there is the simple need to say to all those alive and dead, who make my life both possible and as good as it is, I could never name you all. You are, however, most particularly and personally loved.

Eric Hill Edwards is a member of Sandwich Monthly Meeting and a Recorded Minister in the Religious Society of Friends. Serving on the Committee for the Revision of Faith and Practice Of New England Yearly Meeting since the committee was formed, he has written variously about Quaker matters including two pieces on George Fox documents held in the Swarthmore Manuscripts. Currently, his main interest in Quaker Studies is the radical nature of Quaker worship and its implications for the conduct of a Quaker life. *Quaker Minims* records some of his worship experience.

Living in Falmouth, Massachusetts, in the house he grew up in, Eric H. Edwards' most recent book is *Black Apple, Collected Prose Poems 1975-2022*, also published by One Bird Books.